Job

Interviewing
From
Both Sides

Includes

Proven Interviewing Techniques

and

Detection of Deception Techniques

Wes Wilson

Published by MacDaddy Publishers
Brunswick, GA 31523

Author: Wes Wilson
Senior Editor: Susan Lynn Braswell

You may contact the author at
drweswilson@gmail.com

Table of Contents

Introduction

So, on which side of the desk are YOU sitting for the job interview - - are you hiring or hoping to be hired? Guess what? You can improve the likelihood of getting the very best person for that job opening with your business or (if you are the one seated across the desk) being hired for that dream job if you follow many of the observations and suggestions within the pages of this book!

Ever been involved in a job interview and just could not connect with the other person? Well, you can now, when you learn some of the following techniques that have been used for generations in the law enforcement community.

As a result of my three decades in the field of law enforcement (as a Federal Uniformed Officer, Special Agent, Supervisor and Manager), I have two words that make all the difference for gathering essential information to either hire that best qualified person or to present one's self as being that person that every boss would want to employ.

The secret - - *knowing the elements of an* *effective interviewing*.

Law enforcement personnel are involved daily with conducting interviews in their line of duty activities both with the public and with co-workers. Mix in the officer's own personal and home life communication interactions that directly impact his family as a spouse and/or parent and you have the compelling pressure for developing the verbal ingredients necessary for honing and using convincing communication skills.

Why in the world would you, a boss or person wanting to be hired for a job, desire to learn to interview (or be interviewed) with some of the same skills as a trained law enforcement officer?

Answer – *because these skills work!* They allow you (the interviewer or interviewee) to gather (or give) the most accurate information while utilizing proven questioning techniques. Likewise, you can now learn to be more aware of common behavioral responses demonstrated by the human species.

This will include not only the verbal communications between the sender and receiver but also the *nonverbal messages* being sent.   Certain principles of communication considerations will be addressed; such as question formulation, selecting/creating the environment (for the interview), determining potential times and locations, detecting deception, and using a basic three step process for an interview. I hope you now are getting the idea that these interview techniques, when understood by both parties (interviewer or interviewee) will allow for a better experience for both parties! Will some of this information be too much for you personally? - - Sure! If so, skip it and move on to the next topic of interest and glean what you can use for your own personal situation.

Let's discuss one of the common "elephants in the room" for both parties of the interview - - stress.   Remember when you played a sport and got those "pre-game jitters"?   What happened once you started the first play? - -that nervousness (stress) went away and you reverted to those plays you had practiced backwards and forwards.   Same thing happens in the job interview! If you have knowledge and understanding in the field for which you are hiring/ applying, then all you now have to do is apply some of the techniques that I will be discussing.

So, don't sweat the stress reaction in the job interview; it is a common bodily reaction that is apparent throughout nature – humans are not exempt! These responses are part of the way the human body prepares its senses and muscular abilities to protect itself (and others) from danger or physical threat. The body is preparing for either a "fight or flight" reaction to include physical reactions such as: pupil dilation (which allows more light and better distance vision), quickened breathing (as muscles prepare for that fight or flight they will need more fuel in the form of oxygen), increased heartbeat (to pump this fuel to the farthest extremities), the adrenaline kick (which strengthens the muscles), increased perspiration (to help keep the system cool so that the muscles can work longer and more intensely), and even slowed digestion (so less blood activity is sent to the digestive tract, allowing more flow to the extremities).

So, why should you (interviewer or interviewee) want to be aware of any of these reactions that may be experienced? Answer: by being more attentive to the reactions of yourself (or that person seated across from you), you can more effectively present yourself as representing your company or being the very best person to fill the job opening.

Some stressors are classified as real and others as symbolic. Interviewers, your interviewees will be bringing both to your doorstep, so let make sure you understand the similarities and differences between the two.

Real stress like becoming a victim of a serious crime is different from a symbolic stress that is not as apparently dangerous by itself but becomes harmful to the body because it is cumulative and actually begins to harm the body to a greater degree if left unattended.

Symbolic or internal stresses are those things that one may perceive as having little control of but will affect his life by the way he personally discerns them. The most common of the personal stressors include family, finances, health, and lifestyle. People either interviewing or being interviewed will fall into one, or more likely, both categories of stress. Wouldn't it be helpful to be able to recognize the stress levels of both parties involved in the interview and also become more aware of their sincerity and even their truthfulness?

Stress that is not dealt with can lead to major physical, emotional and interpersonal impacts. Ever wonder why YOU might describe yourself as having frequent bouts with fatigue, hypertension, backaches, headaches, indigestion, even heart disease - - - and seem to be chronically "not feeling well" due to a lowered body resistance? These are prime examples of the typical physical impacts of stress.

Could another person who seems to suffer frequent bouts with depression, anxiety, boredom, anger, guilt, fear, frustration or disappointment be suffering from the emotional impacts of stress? Can interpersonal collisions result in problems, isolation, arguments, cynicism, or violence within and outside of the family unit? The answer to all of these is a resounding, "Yes". Yes, stress affects people physically, emotionally, interpersonally and spiritually. And yes, your stress could easily be detected or projected during that important interview.

An extreme example from my law enforcement career demonstrates chronic stress. Once a cynical correctional officer confided that he knew he was burned out with his job when he witnessed an inmate purposely take a swan dive to his death from a three story prison structure and he, the guard, simply turned to another officer and stated, "I'd give him an 8.5 for degree of difficulty and a 1.5 for entry." This may be an extreme example, or is it that unusual in today's stress packed society? This officer explained that he personally sought counseling after this incident and ultimately left that specific line of work due to the extreme stressors that he could not deal with while being affiliated in the penal system.

So, while seated across from that other person during this interview - - are either of you demonstrating any stressors?

I have mostly interviewed potential hires while on a team of two or three (a procedure followed in the Federal sector). Most potential employees are very cooperative – because they want the job – but some may display reluctance in response to certain questions. If this is the case, before the conclusion of the interview, I would attempt to discover why this person has had a change in attitude.

Interviewers: You should be developing your skills for creating an environment conducive for gaining cooperation through the use of verbal, nonverbal, and symbolic communication. Cooperative and reluctant applicants will offer varying challenges during the actual interview.

CHAPTER ONE

Principles of Interviewing

So, first things first: let's identify principles and methods of preparing for and/or conducting a dynamic job

> *A good interview session should involve focused preparation.*

interview session. Just as one probably doesn't just get up one morning and decide to take a vacation with the spouse and offspring, get in a motorized vehicle and head for that great vacation spot, the interviewer or interviewee should not just show up for this important appointment! This session, when possible, should involve focused preparation.

True or False?
Given the proper atmosphere and a meaningful subject, most people enjoy talking with others.
True,

and it is precisely this same basic principle upon which a great interview is built. Merely talking does not equate with being a good interviewer because effective interviewing is talking with the distinct purpose of eliciting information using a variety of known techniques.

> *Effective interviewing is talking with the distinct purpose of eliciting information.*

The interviewer (and to a lesser degree the interviewee) will be receiving a variety of information (verbal and nonverbal) and will have to mentally analyze all of the contents for accuracy. Some responses will be emotionally laden and will have to be filtered through the interviewer's personal value system and then processed through his training and life experiences.

Let's consider some of the elementary concepts of interviewing: The interview itself is conducted for the purpose of gaining information. Use the basic six W's – Who, What, When, Where, Why, and How. (Must be the "w" on the end of how!) Getting answers to these six questions will provide plenty of information to fully conduct the interview session.

A successful interviewing experience is directly related to the interviewer's specific planning for the upcoming encounter. It is critical to plan ahead for any scheduled interviewing event. What information is already known? (If you have access to the application/resume, read it thoroughly prior to the interview.) Based on available information, what other facts will need to be gathered from this individual? A prepared interviewer will have created a topic outline that gives the name and identifying data regarding the interview: date, time and place of interview including names of persons actually involved in the interview. Is the interview going to be a one-on-one (interviewer and the interviewee), or several interviewers and one interviewee?

Some general rules of conduct for a traditional law enforcement interview can be applicable to any job interview. When an alleged crime has been committed, the law enforcement officer attempts to interview in this order: 1. Victims, 2. Witnesses and 3. Suspects. The reasoning for this order is to gather as much accurate and dependable information from the first two categories of people before confronting the suspects with the case that has been developed, saving the prime suspect for the last interview. In the realm of a job interview, the interviewer, likewise, will have contact with the primary party that is seeking the specific job. Generally speaking, this person should be cooperative (versus reluctant or hostile as is the case in many law enforcement situations) and should be in a physical setting that will be the most conducive for gathering information. The time and place of the interview should be made convenient for both the interviewee and the interviewer but will most frequently be conducted at the interviewer's location.

Unlike a law enforcement interview, where the interview might be conducted on the interviewee's "turf" with the assistance of a second officer, this choice of physical setting would not be recommended for a job interviewing session. The perception of impropriety might tarnish the reputation of both parties! Remember, most of the time, the interviewee has sought the job position (and the interview). Set a formal time for the interviewee to come to the interviewer's office where other staff members will be in the general vicinity.

There should be a conscious attempt to eliminate communication barriers such as desks, crossed arms, etc. The temperature of the room should be comfortable with adequate lighting to create a pleasing environment.

> *There should be a conscious attempt to eliminate communication*

Let's discuss the impact of crimes on possible interviewees. In the law enforcement arena it can be called an awareness of victims and witnesses. If the interviewer's employment is such (convenience store, pizza store, retailer) that an employee is more likely to be robbed or victimized read the information concerning Crisis Reaction covered later in the book. If the interviewee indicates he has been a victim of a crime while working at another business, these tips could assist you in evaluating where he is in the PRAY Model. One of the primary duties of an interviewer is to demonstrate a professional appearance for the business by utilizing a variety of methods to gather information about a potential co-worker. If a person has been a victim or witness to a crime, then one obvious but important aspect of getting to the information may be sidetracked by the emotional impact of the event on the interviewee. The interviewer needs to realize when he conducts an interview, especially the first one, which some interviewees will be suffering from emotional distress, and their ability to provide complete and accurate information is impaired. The last experience desired is to cause this person to be victimized again by the interviewer's lack of knowledge in regards to understanding and using specific communication skills for this type of person. By being able to fine tune your interviewing skills to determine that a potential employee may be still dealing with emotional traumas a result of being a victim or witness to a crime at a previous workplace - - you may actually be interviewing a person who would be the very best for that job because of the experiences he has already had and other potential hires have not yet had!

Law enforcement officers are trained in how to approach victims/witnesses because of the unique emotional impact the crime may be having on these people. As a result of my experience as a law enforcement officer/investigator and trainer, I feel comfortable characterizing the four separate stages involved in the process of resolving a victim or witness' crisis due to a crime. This process is called the PRAY Model of Crisis Reaction. The interviewer can better understand where the interviewee is coming from by thinking of a traumatic event in his own or a close family member's life, and then

> *The four stages of the PRAY Model of Crisis Reaction are:*
> **1. Pivotal**
> *2. Relive*
> *3. Actualization*
> *4. Yearning*

recall how he was personally impacted emotionally, physically and/or mentally.

The first stage of this process is the **Pivotal** Stage. During this stage a person is attempting to distinguish between reality and fantasy. (What is happening?) Some of the more common characteristics of the stage are disbelief, disorientation, confusion, shock (numbness), helplessness, difficulty in recalling details, etc. The first responder (police officer, EMT, police chaplain, firefighter, etc.) will most likely deal with victims and witnesses during this first stage, which lasts from the moment the crime occurred to several days (or more) afterwards. Remember, this is a person who moments before the incident was functioning like he would any other day, and suddenly, now, his world is turned upside down. This person's initial reactions could be as impacted as survivors/witnesses/family members from such memorable criminal/terrorist events as: Sandy Hook Elementary School in Newton, Connecticut (massacre of 26 school children and adult staff—gunned down), Boston Marathon bombings (270+ wounded or killed) or 9/11 (over 3,000 killed by hijacked airplanes).

In law enforcement, the uniformed officer will likely be the first contact for the person in the Pivotal stage. It is not very likely a job interviewer would be conducting the job interview this soon after the interviewee has been victimized.

In all likelihood, the interviewer could be meeting with a job seeker in the **Relive** stage of the PRAY Model of Crisis Reaction. This is the second of four stages and is most common for persons who have had an opportunity to *think about* the recent incident. Let's say you have a clerk job opening at an establishment and your interviewee previously worked in a similar position and had been robbed at gunpoint - - might that be reflected in some of the responses

> *The four stages of the PRAY Model are:*
> 1. *Pivotal*
> **2. Relive**
> 3. *Actualization*
> 4. *Yearning*

(verbal and nonverbal) during the interview?

So, what makes the Relive stage different from the initial Pivotal stage? Some of the more common characteristics of the Relive stage include intense anger or resentment, extreme fear, shame or guilt, and a phobia towards a certain time of day or day of the week (which duplicates the time and day of the event). The phobia might also extend to a specific type of person similar to the criminal. This period of time can last days or months, depending on the severity and type of criminal activity. The family member of a murder victim will certainly be more impacted than the family member of a vehicle theft. The intensity of the reaction of being victimized will be dependent on the severity of the particular incident. The victim's thinking is often focused on attempting to understand why the crime took place and how it affected him personally. Think again, how would this interview applicant fit in at your business if still dealing with some of these traumas?

Some people may feel shame for not doing enough to stop the event or for not spending more time with the victim, etc. This second stage can be an emotional roller coaster from feeling secure to reliving the event with all the terror and lack of control that was experienced initially. The intensity of emotions (moods) may actually be heightened during this second stage when compared to the actual event. Feelings from apathy to anger or calmness to anxiety are not uncommon if the event is perceived as a significant one to the interviewee. These points in time will assist the interviewer in developing communications that will allow the gathering of better information about the interviewer's ability to perform a specific job.

> *The four stages of the PRAY Model are:*
> *1. Pivotal*
> *2. Relive*
> **3. Actualization**
> **4. Yearning**

The final two stages are **Actualization and Yearning** and have been combined due to their close relationship. As the names implies, the interviewee (if a victim or a witness) has reached the emotional state of realistically actualizing again or anew. The feelings of fear or rage will have diminished. The interviewee is thinking and talking less and less about the crime. If the feelings and reactions of the interviewee have been recognized by the interviewer and questions have been answered that might indicate the ability to perform the tasks of the available job, then move on to other areas of questions. For all of us, since stress is cumulative and literally builds from one day to the next, recognition is the first period of behavior in dealing with and eliminating daily stressors. The inability to recognize and aptly unburden oneself of these feelings will result in creating mental barriers for a healthy lifestyle. Do not hold it against an interviewee if he has been a victim or witness to a crime - - it was not his choice!! Just become more understanding that he may have some hurdles to cross and once successfully completed could very likely become one of your best employees. If you are the interviewee and read this section, you may better understand why you have been behaving differently since the incident that made you a victim or a witness. You might also consider whether it would be beneficial to share information concerning your experience with the interviewer.

Notes............Thoughts............Ideas

Chapter One
Principles of Interviewing

An interviewing session should involve focused _____.

Effective interviewing is talking with a distinct purpose of eliciting

_____.

List the six W's:

1.

2.

3.

4.

5.

6.

Name three communication barriers:

1.

2.

3.

Which stage of the PRAY Model is most common for persons who have had an opportunity to think about the recent incident?

Notes............Thoughts............Ideas

_____

_____

_____

_____

_____

_____

_____

_____

_____

_____

_____

Notes............Thoughts............Ideas

_____

_____

_____

_____

_____

_____

_____

_____

_____

_____

_____

CHAPTER TWO

The Interview

Let's establish the importance of active listening (for both parties) before covering any other aspects of the interview process. At the meeting with the job applicant, the interviewer can use certain terms or statements so that the interviewee knows he is actively listening to him. "Tell me about......" is a good structure for creating an atmosphere for gathering a lot of information with one simple question. This is the most prominent way for the interviewer to start determining what, if any, barriers (verbal or nonverbal) may be blocking open communications. Validation of honest feedback such as, "I hear what you are saying" helps create an environment to reduce the stress of the actual interview itself. This also reinforces that the interviewer does have

It is important that the interviewee understand that the interviewer has a process for the time spent.

a process for the time to be spent in the interview as explained at the very beginning after the first introductions of the parties involved.

The actual interview process is based on a simple model that has three steps. I have named this specific process IQ's - - no not an intelligence quotient designed to assess intelligence but a simple acronym to make remembering this interview model easier! By using these three steps of the IQ's, the interview is based on the premise of keeping the conversation structured and consistent. An interviewer must consciously attempt to prepare and conduct all interviews using the same process so all interviewees can be judged by the same standard. The purpose and design of this three step process is to conduct an efficient interview that is both well organized and professional.

This type of interviewing technique allows for a controlled and systematic method of retrieving information. It is designed to give the interviewer confidence by knowing the general order of the interview.

In many job interviews, the interviewer will normally be by himself. If, however, there are two interviewers we will consider the responsibilities of each person in the two person interview. But, first things first, the three steps of the interview process are:

1. **Introduction** 2. **Questions**
3. **Summary** Now, that doesn't look so difficult and it really isn't, but it does take an understanding of the specific steps and practice to become an accomplished interviewer.

The primary interviewer is responsible for establishing control of the interview, to include the Introduction (Step #1) and Questioning

> *The three steps of the IQ Interview Process are:*
>
> *1. Introduction*
> *2. Questions*
> *3. Summary*

(Step #2). The secondary interviewer initially takes a passive role in the interview, by taking notes of what is being verbally spoken and any non-verbal reactions that seem notable, and planning additional strategies or questions. Once the primary interviewer turns the interview over to the secondary, then the secondary will follow up with pertinent questions to retrieve missing information and then summarize (Step #3) the highlights of the interview. Note-taking is a very important part of any successful interview because the notes will become a permanent part of the interview event. The primary interviewer will now make a closing statement, verifying that all parities (interviewee, primary and secondary interviewers) have pertinent contact information so that future meetings can be arranged.

As many job interviews are conducted by a single interviewer, the interviewer must consider whether or not to take notes. If he decides taking notes would be beneficial, the next thing to consider is the most appropriate method of note-taking and when to take those notes. Experience has indicated that it is best not to take any notes until the complete story has been stated by the interviewee. Then, taking notes may be utilized to verify what the interviewer *thinks* he heard. This is a great way to make sure both the interviewer and interviewee are congruent in understanding concerning not only the general themes (of the interview) but the specifics of the interview that ultimately makes it unique within itself.

Step #1 is called the **Introduction** and will likely be the first meeting between you and the interviewee. This will be the time that the first impression is made, and the old adage about "a first impression being a lasting impression" is so true. You do have only one opportunity to make that first good impression, so make the most of it.

The three steps of the interview process are:

1. Introduction
2. Questions

Needless to say, as an interviewer, you are a professional and held to a higher standard of conduct. Due to your unique position as the job interviewer likely possessing the power to recommend (or actually hire) a certain interviewee for the open position, you must maintain fairness throughout this complete process. The interviewer will also be gathering information, at times very personal information, which should be protected and shown great respect. This is why the interviewer should be held to a higher standard of conduct and must demonstrate, through his personal behaviors, both on and off duty, that he is worthy of this responsibility. The interviewer should never discuss an interviewee's personal information with anyone who is not involved in the hiring process. Treat this discussion period/interview situation as one of trust; show respect and consideration for the interviewee.

> *The interviewer will be gathering information which should be protected and shown great respect.*

The Introduction phase of the interview process is used to introduce the interviewer and the interviewee. How embarrassing not to be talking to the person he thinks he is to interview!!! As a former investigator, I had to routinely conduct door knocking interviews (going into neighborhoods or businesses) attempting to locate someone who might have information about the subject of the investigation. Imagine how confusing it would be to ask questions of a person in a neighborhood and use the wrong subject's name. Make sure, especially for the first meeting, that the interviewee's name and appointment time have been verified

One of the major factors of consideration under the Introduction phase is the **purpose of the interview**. This is fairly simple since the interviewer knows that this person (interviewee) desires to work at this business, company, etc. The interviewer could state a purpose such as "I understand you are interested in becoming employed by our ..."

Generally, the interviewer or his representative will have personally initiated the request for this first interview session. This being the case, the introduction can simply be a statement that a time was scheduled for him to spend time discussing the interviewee's potential hiring.

Let's discuss one of the most important elements of a successful interview - - Rapport. Just what in the world is this and why should it be used throughout the entire interview process? If the interviewer will think about those positive experiences he has had interacting with people (maybe a sales clerk, supervisor or even a politician), then think of a negative experience, he might be able to figure out one of the factors that made it a good feeling versus a bad one? Very often, it is the degree of rapport that was established during the interaction.

So what is rapport? Rapport is developing a harmony between persons. Some of the more obvious methods of building rapport would include the words that are spoken, as well as the tone and the inflection. Do the words include warmth or chilliness? What about that tone, is it friendly or condescending? Rapport should be interwoven throughout the entire interview, it is not just a one shot rehearsed smile, word or action and then

Rapport is developing a harmony between

tossed away not to be injected again into the conversation or meeting.

As a retired law enforcement officer I could generally pick out a phony baloney from a mile away, and so can many interviewees/interviewers! Is the interviewer truly glad to have this opportunity to meet with this person or is he just doing his job and will be going through the motions as he deals with the interviewee's application? Good rapport goes a long way toward assisting in gathering information and keeping the interviewee in a friendly and helpful emotional state, but it must be received as genuine in nature. All of these suggestions can work also from both parties' point of view!

Establishing rapport is the most important and often most difficult step in the interview process. If rapport is not established, there will be little chance of building that needed foundation for trust.

The interviewee needs to know that the interviewer is a trustable person.

The interviewee needs to feel that the interviewer is a trustable person who desires to best represent his company while gathering the needed information. The interviewer should not display a military "boot camp" attitude that the interviewee is a worthless, incorrigible person who is only wasting his valuable time! Not many folks would want to work for a boss/business like that!

A good technique is to establish a baseline behavior that places the interviewee at ease by discussing a non-threatening topic of interest. This allows the interviewer to readily identify any changes in the interviewee's behavior as the interviewing session progresses. It is best to attempt not to begin specific sensitive questioning until the person appears to be somewhat relaxed, friendly and desiring to disclose information that will be necessary to develop and ultimately complete the session.

The interviewer should not feel rushed to complete the interview (within obvious limits - - such as other scheduled interviews) until all information has been discovered. Nervousness and anxiety can easily result if the interviewee feels that the clock is running and may likewise, not be willing to share information that is somewhat arduous to discuss.

Step #2 of the interview process involves **Questions**. Now, this is the designated stage for the interviewer to find out what's going on with the interviewee. This is singularly the most important aspect of the interview process. It is during this stage that the interviewer's patience and preceding techniques (Introduction and Rapport) will pay off.

> *The three steps of the interview process are:*
>
> *1. Introduction*
> **2. Questions**
> *3. Summary*

Interviewing/Questioning follows a process that begins with:

(1) *Asking* an open-ended question that allows the interviewee to

> *The question process:*
> *1. Ask*
> *2. Receive*
> *3. Evaluate*

respond in a narrative manner. A simple question such as, "Tell me why you want to work for our organization?"

(2) **Receiving** the answer without interrupting the interviewee. This may seem difficult (not interrupting) but a successful interviewer does not want to distract the flow of information once the information is being given. He can show interest with head nods and slight verbal acknowledgements (that he is tuned in) such as "yes", "uh-huh", etc. Being focused on both the interviewee's verbal and nonverbal communications is important throughout the interview process.

(3) **Evaluating** (verbal, nonverbal or written responses) for truth and consistency. Is the interviewer aware of information that may dispute what the individual is telling him? Are there any discrepancies between earlier comments and current ones? By reviewing any notes (and memory recall) if there were any past meetings, the interviewer will be more knowledgeable should an inconsistency occur.

(4) *Recording* for a permanent record. The best rule is to delay any note taking until the interviewee completes the area of the question asked. It is then and only then that the interviewer should begin to write the highlights of the interview. Otherwise, if note taking begins the moment that the interview session starts, the interviewer would not have the opportunity to evaluate all communications (verbal as well as nonverbal). As we will discuss later, nonverbal communications will reveal a tremendous amount of information about a person.

Should there be the luxury of a second interviewer present for the interview then certain responsibilities are assigned to the primary (lead) interviewer and others to the secondary interviewer. For example, the primary interviewer will ask the initial questions while constantly watching the nonverbals (checking for inconsistencies between the two – verbal versus nonverbal). The secondary interviewer does not interrupt the primary (this could break the train of thought for both the primary interviewer and the interviewee) but waits to ask any questions until the primary turns the interview over to him for the summary. So often, the secondary may think that he has a question that is very important to the line of questioning, but does not realize that the primary interviewer has developed a strategy that will result in the covering of that material.

Good interviewing techniques include starting the interview with general questions and then proceeding to specific questions. Personal background information or non-threatening topics are normally covered first in an effort to put the person more at ease. It is recommended that the interviewer have the person simply respond to open ended (tell me about) questions that pertain to the job opening. Then the job interviewer can go back and dissect the earlier information and continue on with very specific questions based on those previous responses. A common

Good interviewing techniques include starting the interview with general questions and then proceeding to specific

denominator for a good interviewer is to be an attentive listener. The ancient philosopher Epictetus would remind all interviewers that God had a reason for giving us two ears and only one mouth. A trained interviewer must be an attuned listener so that he can properly gather information to help make a hiring decision. Listening requires the accurate perception of what is being communicated. Time must be utilized to properly mentally process the information received from the interviewee. Good listening techniques allow this to occur.

O.K., so what are good/effective questions? Beyond the general tell me type questions, success will be experienced with what are called specific or direct questions, questions that are used to gain further information or more exacting details. Use what is referred to as the "6 W's": the "who", "what", "when", "where", "why", and "how". Try to use positive questions rather than ones that are worded in a negative fashion. "What else do you remember about your job at your previous employment?" is the perfect example of an appropriate question. A negative question that gets the interviewee off the hook would include a response such as: "You can't remember anything else about your previous employment, can you?" The positive type of question is meant to illicit a thoughtful response and may prevent the individual from giving a simple "yes" or "no" for an answer. A backward reaching question is designed to elicit a better recall from the interviewee by placing him back to a specific point in time (such as graduation of high school, etc.) and continuing on from there. "You said that you had been employed as an accountant from February 1998 until 2012 but you have no employment listed since then, what have you been doing since the last job?" Another one could be; "Let's go back to when…"

Praising the interviewee for his efforts is a very effective strategy to use when a roadblock suddenly appears and the conversation seems to stall. Comments like: "You are doing great, now try to discuss…", or "I know that talking about this part of the interview might be difficult, so please take your time".

Statements such as these are supportive and encouraging to individuals who are nervous, upset, or scared and will assist in continuing to build the rapport and trust that is needed throughout an interviewing session.

An opinion question allows the interviewee to offer the interviewer information that is not fact but a notion as to what occurred. Since most people seem to have an opinion about everything from politics to religion, an opinion question will allow information to flow between the sender and receiver of the messages.

What types of questions should be avoided by the interviewer? Does it really matter how questions are framed? Absolutely! The goal is to receive clean (unsoiled) information but certain types of questions will not allow that objective to be achieved.

The **leading** question tends to suggest an answer. For example: "Was your previous job really boring?" Or, "Did you see your former co-worker steal the products at the store?" Leading questions should never be used because human beings are easily swayed by the power of suggestion. The interviewer may not receive the accurate information needed, hence missing the opportunity to receive detailed information that the interviewee would have ultimately relayed if not led to an incorrect conclusion.

The **negative** question is similar to the leading question as it seems to suggest an answer or imply that the interviewer does not want a particular answer. For example, "You didn't get the name of the person who told you about this job opening did you?" The focus should be to keep the interview framed as a positive experience by using questions that allow the interviewee to respond without being influenced by the interviewer. An example would be; "What is the name of the person who gave you the information about this job?"

A **compound** question is asking more than one question at a time, or attaching multiple questions together as only one question. The news media reporters are prime examples of using this technique when attempting to gather as much information as they can when questioning dignitaries (such as the President, etc.) at news conferences. This is not a good technique to use during a job interviewing session as it may only confuse the interviewee and keep the conversation from having a natural flow. Instead of asking, "What other types of jobs did you have at your last company, which one did you like best, who were all your supervisors and did you have health insurance?" A better question would be to simply ask, "Tell me about your other positions at your last employment." Then, if necessary, go back to ask those specific "6 W's" questions!

When compound questions are asked, most people will forget the first question(s), to include the interviewer! Only the last portion of the string of combined questions will generally be addressed. This prevents viable information from being brought to light and discussed. Asking compound questions also allows the interviewee to answer only the question he wants to answer or feels comfortable answering, thus, slowing down the interviewing process.

As previously stated, a good rule of thumb is to go from general questions to specific questions. General questions are the broad (open-ended, "tell me", type) questions; whereas, specific questions narrow down the response to very precise information. "You told me that you worked for your brother Bill till last June; tell me where you were employed after that date." The interviewer can readily surmise that the information gathered from general to specific questions allows the pieces of the puzzle to start coming together.

Good questioning techniques can make the difference between a positive or negative outcome for the interviewing session. The interviewer should remember to use a conversational manner wherever possible, and to use pauses to his advantage. A pause

> *Good questioning techniques can make the difference between a positive or negative outcome for the interviewing*

allows the interviewee to mentally review what has been said and realize that additional comments are needed. A pause can create a degree of uneasiness, so realize that some stress may materialize from it. Watch for verbal and nonverbal indicators of truthfulness and/or deception while striving to build and maintain a positive rapport throughout the entire process

> *Avoid using:*
> *leading questions*
> *negative questions*
> *compound questions*
>
> **Doing so may compromise the integrity of information and limit the amount and type of information that will be beneficial to the interviewing process.**

> *The three steps of the interview process are:*
>
> *1. Introduction*
> *2. Questions*
> **3. Summary**

Note: The **last remaining step of the interview process** will be discussed later in **Chapter Three** when that material is more appropriately covered.

Chapter Two
Notes.............Thoughts.............Ideas

_____

_____

_____

_____

_____

_____

_____

_____

_____

_____

_____

_____

_____

Chapter Two
The Interview

What is validation of honest feelings?

Explain what incorporates the
Introduction in the three steps of the
interview process.

Define rapport.

Who is a phony baloney?

Explain Asking, Receiving, Evaluating and Recording (of the interviewing process).

Good interviewing techniques include starting the interview with general questions and proceeding to _____ questions.

What did the Greek philosopher Epictetus mean about the purpose of God giving man "two ears and only one mouth"?

Why would empathetic responses by the interviewer be used?

Tell how to overcome a roadblock in the conversation.

Why would you not want to use a leading question?

Explain why the negative question is not a preferred question to use.

The compound question can be confusing because:

Notes............Thoughts............Ideas

_____

_____

_____

_____

_____

_____

_____

_____

_____

_____

_____

_____

Notes............Thoughts............Ideas

_____

_____

_____

_____

_____

_____

_____

_____

_____

_____

_____

CHAPTER THREE

Assessment of Truthfulness

One of the most important skills that interviewers can develop is the ability to properly assess both the verbal and nonverbal behaviors of the interviewee during the interview session, since some potential employees will not be completely truthful. With practice and proper training, an interviewer can move from an educated guess to developing skill sets that will allow for a more accurate assessment of those behaviors and speech that are often associated with deception.

> *One of the most important skills that interviewers can develop is the ability to properly assess both the verbal and nonverbal*

Verbal communication involves a variety of considerations as to the accuracy of information that a person may be giving. The interviewer will need to focus on the manner in which the interviewee verbally communicates or responds, as well as what is actually being said. The ability to recognize certain verbal behaviors will assist in determining the truthfulness of the interviewee's statements, and help to indicate the level of stress the individual is experiencing during the interview session. Is there a pattern of significant pauses before answering all questions or just specific ones? Does the individual typically answer a question with a question? Does he repeat the question or does he stammer when answering certain questions about a particular event or incident? All of the above mentioned techniques are used almost naturally with the purpose of increasing a person's response time to a question, which most often results in an untruthful or tainted response.

The interviewer must focus on the actual spoken words, are they congruent with the nonverbal messages? If the words do not agree with the nonverbal reaction, expect discrepancies or problems in the truthfulness of the communication. Listed below are descriptions that will help in making the determination of the truthfulness/deception of information given by an interviewee.

1. Truthful verbal responses tend to be:
   a. Spontaneous (there is little or no hesitation)
   b. Sincere (normal inflection and nonverbal cues)
   c. Direct (very little thought or hesitation – related to spontaneity)
   d. Pronoun usage is present. ("I" or "my" to indicate commitment)

2. Deceptive verbal responses tend to be:
   a. Guarded (interviewee often repeats the question and/or hesitates before answering)
   b. Insincere (response seems methodical or forced)
   c. Evasive (talks around the answer)
   d. Pronoun usage is omitted. ("I" or "my" may become "the").

3. Truthful denials tend to be direct, spontaneous and strong. Normally, the verbal statements from the interviewee who is telling the truth will not be displayed by frail or constrained spontaneity.

4. Deceptive denials tend to produce hesitancy, resulting in the interviewee repeating the question, so that he may have additional time to create a response that is not totally truthful. Listen for generalized responses such as: usually, generally, most of the time. Specific qualifiers will need the interviewer's attention due to common usage that is not allowing the truth to readily surface during the conversation. Such qualifiers are: "I am currently..." or "As far as I can recall....."

Paralinguistics can provide additional resources for the interviewer. Paralinguistics focuses on optional vocal effects to include the tone. The interviewer should be listening for paralinguistic cues that affect the spoken word. Consider any noticeable change in tone and pitch of the voice. Pitch is more responsive to stress because tenseness in the throat will limit the range of pitch. One's tone is likely to increase with anxiety, such as not being fully forthright or truthful. If a person suddenly becomes ambiguous or evasive with answers, an attentive interviewer will put his antennas up and make a mental note as to what topic is being covered.

Certain responses that create a word whisker or sub-vocal are common when one becomes nervous. Examples would include: "uh", "ah", "err", "um", "ok" or a variety of response that will create a moment's delay. The more uncomfortable a person becomes, the greater the frequency of these sub-vocals.

Certain responses that create a word whisker or sub-vocal are common when one becomes

Due to the constant bombardment of avenues of sound (music,

television, etc.) in today's modern society, many people will begin to feel uncomfortable with the sound of silence. Once realized, the interviewer can relieve this stressor by filling in the silence with comments or questions to gently bring the interviewee back into the conversation. However, if it is felt that the person is not being honest with his statements, lengthening the pause might actually create more stress so that the person will be brought around to the truth.

What about the rate of speech and truthfulness? During the building rapport phase of the interview a baseline behavior can be established in regards to the rate of speech. Later in the information gathering phase, the interviewer should listen for changes that could be an indication of nervousness and/or deception. As a general rule, the rate of speech may decrease if a lie is not well rehearsed and the person is creating the story as he goes along. Should the rate of speech noticeably increase, the person may be wishing to get the lie out and attempt to show that he has nothing to hide. The amount of time it takes the person to verbally respond to questions is generally greater when a lie is being formulated versus a lesser time if it has been practiced.

Nonverbal communication is one of the more interesting aspects of interviewing a person that is directly linked to the spoken word. The interviewer should not only be listening to what is being said, but also watching to see if the words agree with or are congruent with the nonverbal communications. Criminal investigators have recognized for some time that it is easier to deceive verbally than it is to do so in a nonverbal way. People have a conscious ability to control what they say versus nonverbal communication which is frequently involuntary. This is due to the physiological (bodily) stress responses over which the person generally has no real control.

> *Nonverbal communication is one of the more interesting aspects of interviewing a*

So what is **body language** and why should an interviewer be concerned about it? Body language is actually the visible reactions to the stress response. What does this mean? The interviewer should listen and watch for stress that may externalize due to deception or embarrassment. It becomes the task of the talented interviewer to determine which one it is (deception or embarrassment) and use this nonverbal behavior as a starting point for drawing conclusions about the truthfulness of the interviewee.

Body language is actually the visible reactions to the stress response.

Since the individual's ability to control verbal cues is greater (and hence less reliable) than controlling the nonverbal cues (which are more reliable), the interviewer needs to focus on those nonverbal cues while the interviewee is speaking. Are the nonverbal cues congruent with the spoken words?

Let's consider four factors that are relevant when evaluating behaviors as indicators of truth or deception during an interviewing session.

1. Culture – Cultural background has a direct influence on one's behaviors. The interviewer should attempt to study and recognize the behaviors that are normal for the interviewee's culture. Having patrolled the areas that intersect with the Cherokee reservation, I learned many of the various cultural differences between those on and off the reservation. An example would be less direct eye contact from a Native American tribe member to the officer. This is also true in many Hispanic cultures where eye contact is often averted as a sign of respect for someone considered in a superior position or position of authority. This person would not necessarily be hiding something but showing respect by not looking directly at the officer, which might be misconstrued as a challenge to the

authority of the law enforcement officer. Consider the same when job interviewing people not from the same background.

2. Change – What if the behavior of an interviewee changes as the questioning progresses? These changes could be due to stress that has developed from the questions being asked or could simply be part of the interviewee's normal behavior pattern. That is why it is recommended that a baseline behavior be established by asking slow pitch (non-threatening) questions at the start of the interview process.

3. Context – Consider the timing of the changes. It is important to ask the question then wait and watch (and listen) for the response. Most deceptive behaviors will occur within the first three to five seconds after the question is asked. Would a person folding his arms across his chest indicate a deception or could it be due to an environmental change such as the

air conditioning coming on and blowing directly on him?

4. Clusters – Do not rely on just a single behavioral cue (response) as being a deciding factor of deception. Most behaviors representing deceptions occur in clusters of two or more behaviors displayed within that three to five second period of time after a stressful question or comment.

It is important to recognize the necessity of not only listening to the interviewee but watching the response. A person's posture and body movement is a good indicator of his actual attitude and allows for important messages, answers or cues to be gathered.

What about postures that may indicate a truthful response versus a deceptive one? It all starts with the observation of the interviewee's sitting position. Authentic statements are usually given by individuals who sit upright and appear comfortable. They will be frontally aligned with the interviewer and often lean forward while appearing interested in the conversation. While some nervousness is normal, the truthful person will appear more relaxed with only slight indications of nervousness. The person will not make dramatic changes in his posturing; in that, it will be a smooth transition as the conversation continues at the same pace from one question/topic to another.

The deceptive person will often sit slouched or huddled in a chair, as a psychological or physical defense to prevent the interviewer from getting close. Often he is not frontally aligned with the interviewer but will turn his hips away from the interviewer. This is a form of blocking any direct contact with the interviewer.

The deceptive person may also demonstrate erratic changes in postures as if he cannot sit still for the conversation. It is when the rhythm of change appears after each question that the truthfulness of the responses should be examined.

If the interviewee demonstrates a body slump with the head down, this is often the surrender position that means he is ready to admit or clarify a misstatement or outright lie. An interviewee in this situation should be allowed to speak uninterrupted. Let him give you the most truthful information he has to offer.

It is recommended that the interviewer show the interviewee to a specific chair so that there are no physical barriers between the two parties (interviewee and interviewer). Sitting behind a desk is considered a position of power but creates a barrier to the interviewee who may already be reluctant about the meeting. Remove barriers to obtain the most factual information!

Check out the position of interviewee's feet, near or under his chair. If both feet are hidden behind or under the chair, this is an indication of deception or stress. What if one foot is behind the chair and the other is placed under the chair like a sprinter in track blocks? It is a reasonable inference that the person really doesn't want to be there and is waiting for the starting pistol to fire so he can race out of your office! Another sign of stress and uneasiness is the tapping of feet or fingers.

Gestures are used to relay a message or make a point. Not only do gestures give commands or orders, such as stop, go, or left turn/right turn, but likewise, the many gestures that another person can give with the body will indicate his moods or intentions.

> *Gestures are used to relay a message or*

What are some of the more noticeable indicators of a person's moods? The head or chin in hand with the head slightly cocked shows lack of interest. Holding the head straight shows interest. The crossing of arms, legs and ankles indicates a closed posture or being defensive, trying to keep the other person away to protect one's space. The hiding of one's mouth or eyes is often an indicator of trying to hide something or prevent it from coming out. Ever have a child spew a spontaneous utterance ("I don't know why I said it, it just came out!") and then quickly cover his mouth or dart his eyes to the floor? Attitudes and emotions are expressed mainly in the face. Reading (examining) the interviewee's face allows the interviewer to determine the interviewee's attitude towards the interviewer, others, or a specific situation.

In law enforcement, if the officer can observe a person for a baseline behavior, he can often better understand that person, then move to the next step of predicting a behavior and, ultimately, gaining some control over the outcome of the interaction.

Recognition of behaviors is the first step in responding accurately to a person's intentions or actions. Knowledge equals understanding!

Recognition of behaviors is the first step in responding accurately to a person's intentions or

During a job interviewing session, information can be gleaned by observing the types of **body lean** that a person displays. Each of the three common styles or positions of the lean has a corresponding effect, intent or message for the interviewer.

1. The **forward lean** is a positive response and indicates that the person is attentive and interested in what the interviewer is saying.
2. The **upright lean** is neutral and shows that the person is listening to the information but may not be giving a true reading of interest or disinterest.
3. The **rearward lean** is a negative response which exhibits a lack of interest, retreating from the information or topic of the discussion. Hostility can also be perceived from this stance.

The interviewer will normally have an opportunity to observe the **ambulation** of the interviewee as he comes into the office. A person's walk can tell volumes about his emotional outlook. Many younger adults think the primary observable characteristic of what makes a person "old" is the way he walks. Does the person's walk project vigor or an ambling from one spot to another?

The walk of a person shows the inner confidence of the person, or lack thereof. Minus a physical handicap that impedes a person's ability to walk with a normal gait, various signals can be sent regarding his own perceived confidence, sense of accomplishment, cautiousness or even insecurity. Does the interviewee enter the room with a bounce of self-assuredness or does he appear with slumped shoulder, no eye contact and almost dragging himself to the office? The way we walk indicates a multitude of information about us!

> *Proxemics is the study of space and distance and the impact it has between individuals.*

Proxemics is the study of space and distance and the impact it has between individuals. Space is a very important communications consideration in any interviewing situation. Just as one's territory is designated by yards, fences, posted signs "keep out", a human also marks his territory by creating and maintaining a personal space (zone) around himself. Zones are directly dependant upon specific situations.

79

There are four recognized zones for interaction in our modern day Western society.

1. *Intimate* (zone) is from 0 to 18 inches and is reserved for special people such as a spouse, child or another loved one. It could be used to comfort someone who has experienced a death or shocking event.
2. *Personal* (zone) is from 18 inches to 4 feet and is used for situations that involve persons that are familiar with one another such as good friends.
3. *Social* (zone) is from 4 to 12 feet and would be used for interactions in business, meeting new acquaintances or even standing and waiting while someone uses the ATM.
4. *Public* (zone) is from 12 to 20 feet and is reserved for strangers and activities where one desires the maximum distance before any encounter. Fans of athletes or a candidate making a political

speech would generally be in this area.

An interview can be started in any of the four previously mentioned zones, but most are conducted in the social zone. Remember that invading one's personal space can raise anxiety and create an environment that is not positive for a friendly discussion. Law enforcement interviewers typically conduct interviews at a closer range to **create distress** if the person shows signs of unwillingness to cooperate so that he can then be covertly rewarded by increasing the personal space once information is forthcoming. But, in a job interviewing session, the goal is to **create a secure** environment in which the interviewee will be at ease and desire to share information; therefore, be aware of and respect the interviewee's space so that he will be comfortable enough to communicate openly.

Touch or **Haptics** is greatly influenced by the culture from which a person has been programmed. A male from a Middle Eastern country would expect to come so close as to smell your breath which is within the intimate zone of 0 to 18 inches. Most Americans would feel very uncomfortable with someone invading this space and would start backing away. This could create a clash of cultures with the Middle Eastern person wondering why he is not wanted that close and the American thinking that the other person is very forward, likely resulting in hostility or rejection in regards to communication with this person. Other contact cultures would include the Hispanic and Turkish cultures. Cultures that traditionally have less touch would include much of northern Europe and many Asian cultures. Even within the United States, the use and acceptance of touch is more acceptable in one region of the country than another. The Deep South is known for its friendliness and willingness to "hug your neck". Those that study American History would recognize that the New Englander President, Calvin Coolidge, was the recipient of many jokes (during and after his administration) due to his stereotyped stoic demeanor.

speaker is finishing his remarks and it is now his turn.

The interviewee's eyes will reveal pertinent nonverbal behaviors if the interviewer is aware of what to look for during the session. **Sanpaku** is Japanese for three whites which refers to the three whites showing (below and on each side of the pupil) and is normally an indication of extreme stress. Beware of interpreting too much from this technique as medical or physical conditions may also cause this physical response. The interviewer should also be attuned to whether or not he has a good angle towards the person's head and eyes.

Another method of determining the stress/deception in a person at any given time is to monitor his eye blinks per minute (bpm). One's blinking rate can increase greatly when under stress, particularly prolonged stress. The normal rate is approximately 13-15 bpm. There is a report that Saddam Hussein had a normal bpm of 13 shortly before the Iraqi war but one week into the war the rate skyrocketed to 130 bpm.

Also consider that when the interviewee breaks eye contact that this could suggest stress or deceit regarding a specific line of questioning. The closing of eyes, covering the eyes with hands, diverting the eyes away from the interviewer, or the raising of the eyebrows could all be characterized as indicators of stress or deceit.

By being truly attuned to the interviewee's physical responses to the conversation, the attentive interviewer should attempt to determine if the carotid pulse is increasing as the blood is pulsating up the neck to the head as this is another indicator of stress or deceit. Closely related to this would be the pace and breathing rate of the person. Is the breathing fast, slow, medium, with pauses or various rhythms? When breathing shifts in rhythm or in body placement, there is a reason! Additionally, the interviewer must make an attempt to determine why there is a change in the individual's natural exchange of oxygen and carbon dioxide.

A person's facial expressions relate to the emotions they are inwardly experiencing at any given time. Focus on the mouth to notice tension which may create dry mouth indicated by the licking of the lips or the clicking sound of the tongue caused by the mouth itself suddenly becoming dry. Often people delivering false information will cover their mouth in some fashion, as if this will somehow block their deceptive language from reaching the interviewer's ears. A smile can mask emotions and may show nervousness if sent at an inappropriate time during the conversation.

The nose is extremely stress-sensitive therefore it should be notated if an interviewee starts to rub his nose during a specific area of any questioning or conversation. This, again, is why establishing that base line behavior at the beginning of an interview is imperative. Later, any departure from that normal behavior should be noticed. When establishing this norm, consider the context of the environment and the intensity of the setting.

Due to the sensitivity of the human hair, a person may scratch his head during a stressful situation such as telling a lie. The pilo-erection of the hair itself will cause one to scratch the hair; so watch the interviewee's hand movements, particularly towards his head or nose.

Don't forget to also view the interviewee's upper body and look for tension. Notice any increase in the overall level of movement and gestures with the interviewee's neck, shoulders, arms and hands. Any overt variances should be noted in reference to the precise line of questioning as this will assist in understanding the truth of the conversation.

It is your looking, listening and even sensing that allows you to notice changes by the individual you are involved with during any job interviewing

Remember that it is your looking, listening and even sensing that allows you to notice and track patterns of repetition and rhythms so that you can better recognize changes by the individual you are involved with during any session.

Steps one and two of the interview process were covered in Chapter Two. This is a good time to complete the discussion of the final phase of this process. Step #3 (of the interview process) is the **Summary**. If there is only one interviewer (as is the case in many job interviewing situations), the process of summarizing the information derived from the meeting is obviously a very important part of the interview.

Not only are you confirming general highlights of the interview but also those most relevant nuggets that will likely reap benefits (remember, you went from general to specific questions during the interview). It is during this stage that most interviewees will want to clarify, correct, or add to previously discussed matters. The summary allows the interviewer to clear up any hurried or unclear topics and verify his own

89

recordings in the notes. Also, be sure to specifically ask the interviewee if the summary sounds accurate to him and ask if he can think of anything else that might benefit his interview.

"The weakest ink is stronger than the best memory." That statement speaks volumes for the need for accurate note taking so that future involvements with the interviewee (maybe a follow-up interview) will have errorless accounts of where you have been and help lead you to where you want to go.

Should you be fortunate enough to have a second interviewer present, then the summary should be conducted by this secondary individual. This is now the opportunity for the secondary to ask any questions he feels should have been asked by the primary interviewer. After these follow-up questions then he may go directly into the summary stage.

For confidentiality purposes, all notes should be maintained in a secured location with only your accessibility. All sessions will then be properly recorded and secured for future use.

Step #3 (Summary) will include a closing and is the last pertinent element of our interviewing process. Just as you would conclude a conversation with a family member or friend on the street or the telephone, you need to close out the interview by following a few simple guidelines.

It is important that the interviewee felt welcomed (part of the rapport that we discussed earlier) during the interviewing session, so simply thank him for the opportunity that both of you have just experienced. The interviewer should advise the interviewee if the position may require an additional interview.

The interviewee should know how to contact you or a staff member if additional information has been requested. Likewise, you need to know how to contact the interviewee should you have to need more information or an additional meeting.

91

As the job interviewer, you must decide how important it is to detect deception during an interviewing session. If you recognize that the interviewee is engaging in deception, intentionally hiding the truth, then you must decide how to approach finding the truth or just conclude and move on to the next applicant

By having the ability to observe, catalog, differentiate and memorialize human behaviors, you will be better able to deal with people that are not forthcoming with you. Their intention may be to deliberately falsify or omit information to the interviewer to best suit their personal agenda - - gaining the job. Sometimes the deception is simply an attempt to slant the truth in one direction (make the interviewee look better); however, it could be an indication of a much more serious situation. It might be

As the job interviewer, you must decide how important it is to detect deception during an interviewing

helpful to refer to <u>The Diagnostic Manual of Mental Disorders</u> which lists diagnostic criteria for schizophrenia, dementia, delirium, and dissociate disorders, particularly if the job position is of a sensitive nature requiring only persons who are of a trustworthy nature. Your employer may have specialists who could determine any perceived disorder.

Upon meeting a person for the first time, most of us feel comfortable in sizing him up in regards to our own personal experiences and values. Is he open and friendly or does he appear defensive and not interested in interacting? Does he appear strong-willed and become very direct, even forceful, in wanting to dominant a conversation or situation? Has he demonstrated the ability to listen to what you are asking without constantly interrupting you?

So, as a job interviewer, you have a challenge to learn more about your interviewee's personality so you can maintain the professional demeanor expected of someone in your position. How do you increase the likelihood of achieving a better read about an applicant?

The interviewer should train himself to be impartial or unbiased when it comes to dealing with each individual interviewee.

As addressed earlier, people will send out nonverbal cues when they lie. These cues are just natural actions that accompany deceptive communication. Remember that you will evaluate these cues as clusters (with other cues, not just one by itself).

Most people will not distinguish the truth from a falsehood because they are not looking for the right nonverbal signs for the lie. Most of the time people identify lies or actually believe lies based on two principles:

1. Plausibility of the statement.
2. Analysis of the statement and its consistency with previous statements—combined with the background knowledge of the interviewer.

Most people will not distinguish the truth from a falsehood because they are not looking for the right nonverbal signs for the lie.

Notes............Thoughts............Ideas

_____

_____

_____

_____

_____

_____

_____

_____

_____

_____

_____

_____

Chapter Three – Assessment of Truthfulness

Regarding verbal communication, what are some techniques used by an interviewee to increase response time with the likely intention of sending an untruthful response?

List some clues that verbal responses are truthful or deceptive:

Why is it important to establish a baseline behavior of your interviewee's rate of speech, etc.?

Body language is the _____ response to the stress response.

Think of at least two clusters of behavioral clues or responses that can indicate deception.

Recognition of behaviors is the first step in responding accurately to a person's intentions or _____.

The forward lean is considered what type of response?

What is proxemics?

Circle one - -

In mainstream America, it is the
listener   *speaker*   who maintains
the greater eye contact.

Regarding the interviewee's eyes, what
are some actions that may suggest stress
or deceit regarding a specific line of
questioning?

Why is the summary of an interview so
important?

Notes............Thoughts............Ideas

_____

_____

_____

_____

_____

_____

_____

_____

_____

_____

_____

_____

Notes............Thoughts............Ideas

CHAPTER FOUR

Barriers and How to Remove Them

Barriers to effective communications and job interviewing have been discussed but let's consider more barriers that might hinder your conversation. What we desire to do is to identify perceived body barriers of a closed mind that will shut the speaker out, causing resistance to the messages and bringing defensiveness to the situation.

The interviewer must be aware that body barriers can exist coequally for both himself and the interviewee. The interviewer must be able to recognize and remove existing barriers to be an effective communicator. You must be conscious of your own personal behaviors and determine how the job seeker may perceive them.

Authoritarian barriers provide a tremendous hindrance to the communication process. If an interviewee is intimidated by an authoritarian barrier, then the flow of information will not be at the optimum level. There are five common actions or behaviors that could be perceived as being authoritarian.

1. Sitting behind a desk will do it every time. What a physical barrier! **Get out from behind that desk** and drop some of the perceived trappings of your position.

2. Placing the hands on one's hips recalls the memory of when Mother did that and you knew you were in trouble! The interviewee is not in trouble, he is seeking a job!

3. Crossing of arms is perceived as being closed or defensive, so even if you are sitting under an air conditioning vent, don't cross your arms – just move so you will not be cold!

4. Steepling of fingers sends the message of superiority, so even if your personal church has a huge tower/steeple, don't use this

nonverbal unless you are not confident in your own abilities.

5. Superior eye level, such as looking down on the interviewee, will create a barrier to communications. Be sure that your chair is at the same level as your interviewee to prevent this superiority. [During law enforcement interviews, if the previous interview of a suspect to a crime had not resulted in receiving positive, truthful responses, the interviewer would physically sit in a taller chair to send the unspoken message that he was in a position of authority and psychologically in charge. This message would normally create an atmosphere of uneasiness for the suspect and combined with invading the suspect's personal zone (simply leaning toward the suspect) would very likely gain some degree of cooperation. Then subtle rewards would be given back by simply leaning backwards in the chair and creating more distance.] Obviously, a job interviewer will be attempting to eliminate all of the actions that

create any hindrance to the process of retrieving information.

Try to keep in mind that there are numerous other barriers that can negatively impact the free flow of conversation. As a job interviewer you need to be aware of several factors that can impede the interviewing session:

1. Making premature comments or evaluations. "Don't think you have the plot figured out before you see the whole movie" also applies in job interviewing.

2. Interrupting the interviewee - - unless he is just totally rambling. This breaks the natural flow of information and generally takes more time to gather all the facts than allowing the person to give the information once and then going back to dissect and clarify it.

3. Dominating the conversation. Here again, ask the open-ended question ("tell me" type question) and allow the interviewee to fully respond.

What are some of the common barriers to cross-cultural communication that the job interviewer may be dealing with in his local community?

With some of the larger American cities having over 100 cultures living together, it is not realistic to envision having an incisive understanding of all these cultures when it comes to job interviewing. It is through recognizing and showing respect for the various cultures that we can learn how to tear down barriers that will impact the communication process.

One of the primary barriers to cross cultural communications is language. Have you ever traveled to a foreign country (or even a different region of the United States) and simply did not understand what people were saying? Obviously, effective communications will suffer greatly if individuals from different cultures can not understand each other's language. It has been said that facts are mostly communicated by language and other avenues are used to convey feelings. This is why such emphasis is placed on nonverbal communications in the law enforcement communities due to officer safety considerations when dealing with the public. The job interviewer who speaks foreign languages enhances communication when he is also aware of the various cultural norms for a specific country.

A common practice is to refer to nonverbals, such as hand signals, when the spoken word is not getting the message across. But, beware; there are numerous examples where an acceptable hand gesture in one society is quite insulting in another. [While living in England as a child, I soon learned that the "V" for Victory sign (as made famous by Sir Winston Churchill), when reversed, (with the palm turned backwards/outward) is an obscene gesture.] Other cultures find the pointing of the index finger as insulting (symbolic hit/murder sign) or the curled finger motioning to come here as degrading when projected from one human to another.

Another primary barrier to cross cultural communications is the ignorance of various cultural norms. So what would be considered typical traits in the behavior of a social group or country that are handed down from one generation to another? The culture of a country is impacted by the language, religion, economics, climate, geography, etc. There are many differences in cultural behaviors that can be observed throughout the world and even within a country such as the United States. Examples would include punctuality and the concept of time, as in being on time for a set appointment versus "I'll get there when I get there or maybe tomorrow I'll show up".

While an American might want to be direct and cut to the chase involving a business deal or even a conversation, many other cultures, such as Asians, find too much directness rude and offensive. Rather than telling an American an outright "no" they may soften it by saying "maybe" when they, in fact, really do mean "no".

Most people are proud of their given names. The job interviewer will show respect when he can recognize that making incorrect changes or mispronunciations, however slight, may insult or offend the interviewee. It would be wise to ask if you are pronouncing a person's name correctly. By simply asking the correct pronunciation of a person's name you are indicating that you wish to pronounce it correctly. In the mainstream culture of the U.S., an individual may use his first and/or middle names and a single last (surname) name. In the Hispanic culture, more than one given name and several surnames will be more common. Also, compound surnames may also be very frequent. With children, the first element probably is the father's surname, and the second element the mother's. For married women, the last element is the husband's surname. Many Middle Eastern countries use multiple names to signify the family ancestry.

An effective job interviewer will research any and all information at his disposal about the culture of the interviewee prior to the meeting to pave the way to clear communication.

Having knowledge of other world cultures will allow the interviewer to more effectively interact with those not from his own culture. This knowledge will help eliminate prejudices (stereotyping) that seem to prevail in all societies. Intellectually, most people acknowledge that stereotyping is counterproductive because it is just not true! The job interviewer can help break the bonds of ethnocentrism, that one's own ethic group is the superior one.

So, how do we go about improving cross cultural communications? Accepting the reality that today's job interviewer will be dealing with a more diverse society than at any other time in our nation's history, it will be beneficial to make every effort to improve one's personal ability to handle those

> *Having knowledge of other world cultures will allow the interviewer to more effectively interact with those not from his own culture.*

interviewing situations. Just like you have received various formal training opportunities to become a job interviewer, education and other related junctures are important factors to better equip you with the knowledge and ability to meet with applicants not from your primary culture.

Awareness will allow you to better understand the customs, both verbal and nonverbal of a particular culture. As the interviewer you should be accepting of the person's culture from the point of view that he is acting a certain way as a result of his own culture and begin to surmise if this person would make a good employee. You do not have to personally agree with all aspects of another culture but simply attempt to develop a better comprehension of why the person (from that culture) behaves as he does and how that behavior would impact the other employees.

How unbiased can you personally be when dealing with an individual from another culture? **One's personal bias can cause the biggest roadblock** in understanding the other's point of view.

Attempt to understand where this person is coming from as far as his personal experience, imprinting as a child or young adult, etc., and why he may be responding the way he does. Do not treat any one cultural group differently or with any more respect than another.

Another component in effective communication is self-concept. One's own self-concept is the single most determinant that affects one's communicative behavior. This ascertains who we are and how we perceive (filter) or react to our environment. One's self-concept is determined by experiences with meaningful others. A positive, strong self-concept is directly impacted by love, respect, trust, and acceptance. This is just another example of the importance of a loving and nurturing relationship between family members and a child's self-concept; it can not be overstated!

Consider your own self-concept as an interviewer and the way you will be perceived by interviewees. Will you project confidence, professionalism, fairness, honesty, trustworthiness, and empathy? Stating the obvious, if the interviewee does not trust you, the session will not be as productive as desired.

If you are attempting to gather the most relevant information from an interviewee, the interviewer may want to consider the following, particularly if you sense some barriers:

1. Postures and gestures should be similar or matched in a subtle manner so the interviewee is subconsciously recognizing that you are like him. If the interviewee is exhibiting a posture that might indicate a closed position, such as crossing his arms or legs, placing his hand to chin, turning slightly to one side or another, etc., adapt that same posture. Then after holding that pose for a few moments, open your stance to promote open communication. Hopefully, the interviewee will also open his stance and information will flow more freely.

2. Matched breathing rates promote harmony in this relationship of interviewer and interviewee. Simply observe the inhaling and exhaling of the

interviewee's shoulders or chest and attempt to casually match the rhythm of yours to his.

3. Eye blinks are one of the easier physical responses to identify and match. Generally, in a stressful situation, one's eye blinks will be greater and decrease as one begins to feel more comfortable. If it is noticed that the interviewee is under stress, the interviewer might slightly increase his eye blinks, then begin to decrease eye blinks, thus modeling a more relaxed environment.

4. Vocal characteristic include many factors such as: volume, tone of voice, pitch of voice, rate of speed and vocal inflection. These are easily identified by simply listening and responding in a like manner.

5. Body cadence can be matched by the same body variations without making it extremely overt to the interviewee. Foot tapings, swaying or movements can be duplicated by the same rhythm of the interviewee's movement then slowly lessen the intensity of the movement

115

resulting in a calmer interviewee (and interviewer).

Once you are confident and competent to achieve satisfactory results in mirroring (reflecting) the same behaviors, you are ready to actually start directing someone's behavior in a discreet, covert fashion. Remember, this is being done with the highest respect for the individual's uniqueness *with the goal of the interviewee eventually developing a more open attitude to give you the most accurate information.*

When the interviewee is sitting with a closed position (arms/legs folded, sitting in a pointedly erect position with an austere facial expression), the interviewer, after mirroring these behaviors, would discreetly begin to lead the interviewee to a more open position. This is accomplished by slowly unfolding one's own posture (and then change any other closed indicators) to present a more open and trusting positioning. Normally, the interviewee will begin to modify his closed positioning and become more open (physically), which will allow for more forthright communications. This technique appeals to the unconscious level of the person.

The interviewer can positively reinforce the interviewee's attempts to develop self-disclosures by many verbal and nonverbal actions. The use of positive head nods shows attention and engagement. Other techniques include the sincere smile, verbalizations ("I hear you.", "Yes.", "Continue please.", etc.) and sub-vocals ("uh-hum", "ah", etc.)

 Just as a salty peanut can be enclosed or embedded and surrounded closely by delightful chocolate, certain statements or words can have meanings beyond that of the apparent original intent. These types of words or statements (let's call them the **chocolate covered peanut concept**) can actually contain insinuations, questions or even directions and are used in the present tense (of language). The uniqueness of these chocolate covered peanut words or statements is they appear to be referencing the interviewer but actually are directed to the interviewee. These types of statements and words are a part of our everyday language and are nearly unnoticeable but relate to one's subconscious level; therefore, they are less likely to arouse a somewhat resistant interviewee's defensive responses which are common to a command type of questioning.

A **chocolate covered peanut** suggestion will affect the interviewee in a subtle manner and will suggest a specific attitude (change), cooperation, or direction. This suggestion (via words or phrases) would be beyond the intended statement in that it would indicate cooperation, helpfulness, responsibility, or thoughtfulness.   Examples would include: "You seem like a very responsible person." (Who wants to admit they are not responsible?), "I know you want to be as open and forthright as possible." (Even a liar normally wants to be perceived as an honest person.).

> A chocolate covered **peanut** suggestion will affect the interviewee in a subtle manner and will suggest a specific attitude, cooperation or

Another technique that is effective in positively altering the interviewee's behaviors is with the development of questions that assist in a suggestion by using time-related words such as: start, stop, already, previously, still, continually, always, etc.

Sample comment/questions could start something like: "I appreciate your willingness to discuss the topic as to your termination at your last job." or "When would you like to start talking about the event (your termination at your last job)?"

The chocolate covered peanut (embedded questions) can also contain suggestive questions within the larger context of the interview process. An embedded question is more specific than an embedded suggestion and is designed with attributes of directing the interviewee. Some examples would include:

1. "I don't know what you did at your last job that so badly upset you." (What did you see and hear?)

2. "I am attempting to process the order of events of what you said happened to you at your last job." (What did happen to you at your last job?)

3. "It would be interesting for me to know why someone would think that about their previous boss." (Why would you think that about your boss?)

An indirect method for diplomatically commanding or directing the interviewee to divulge information or cooperation is to use a less stressful context of the earlier discussed narrative statement. Example: "Tell me what happened." – direct approach - versus "I would like for you to explain to me what happened." – indirect approach.

Remember that rapport was discussed earlier and is extremely important throughout the interviewing session. Rapport must be developed and nurtured if the initial encounter is to progress with some degree of harmony. Rapport may have to

> *Rapport may have to be resuscitated if emotions get the most of the*

be resuscitated if emotions get the most of the interviewee. This can be accomplished by gently directing him back into a positive behavior. Rapport is marked with developing a harmony between persons. Good rapport goes a long way in assisting the gathering of information and keeping the interviewee in a friendly and helpful emotional state, but it must be received as genuine in nature.

Rapport will help to deflate varying degrees of interviewee resistance. Another proven technique involves building on the rapport aspect and moving on to gaining more cooperation and acceptance (by the interviewee) towards the job interviewer. One specific method to achieve this goal is to format a series of questions that require a "yes" response. These questions will produce agreement so that you can move into more open ended or narrative questioning. Your goal is to have a series of positive responses so that he gets into a rhythm of saying "yes" which aids in deflating his resistance to upcoming areas of questioning where more scrutiny will be placed on the answers received by the interviewer. Car salesmen are generally experts with using this technique to get you in the "yes" mode - - buyers beware!

Are you old enough to have actually seen a shallow well that used a hand pump which had to be primed before a constant flow of water could be received? The principle of *giving a little to get a lot* works in certain interviewing/counseling situations. For example, a interviewee/interviewee may (at first) be very reluctant to discuss the specifics of an event that has personally impacted him. This could be due to fear, shame, guilt or a variety of other unknown reasons. So a technique to get the information flowing is to give permission for the interviewee/client to withhold information that he does not want to discuss (for now). This is similar to our chocolate covered peanut concept using an embedded command with a slight variance. Since the interviewee/client feels more confident that he still has control over the flow of information, he will actually disclose more information than he had intended prior to your giving him permission to withhold uncomfortable factors.

An example: "I would like for you to tell me about the events at your last job that involved your firing, but you do not have to tell me everything. Just tell me what you feel comfortable telling me and don't tell me anything else." (The interviewer is giving permission not to reveal information that may upset the interviewee but has actually inserted five chocolate covered peanut commands to tell me.)

A technique to use to retrieve information from an interviewee who has been a victim or witness to a criminal event and is reluctant to answer questions due to not wanting to experience the incident again is to use **dissociation**. Dissociation alters ones' consciousness resulting in the normal perception of present events. Severe psychological trauma to an event such as being assaulted (victimized) can cause ones' inner core to seek stability from the event by disassociating a connection to it - - extreme cases may involve temporary amnesia.

Close observation of the interviewee is needed during this exercise to make sure that he does not become too uncomfortable during the session. Start by asking the interviewee if he is comfortable and is willing to discuss the previous event. Use of some victim/ witness technique statements like "You are safe now." will assist in creating the positive atmosphere needed. Request that the interviewee now recall the significant event and add any visual, auditory, kinesthetic and/or olfactory remembrances to the occurrence. Finally, have the person describe what he is seeing, hearing, feeling, or smelling. This will allow for potential explicitly unknown or forgotten information to be brought forth for discussion. [This would be more appropriate for a job seeker needing a highly classified security clearance.]

Should you decide that an interviewee is being purposely uncooperative and/or attempting to deceive you, there are subtle but potent signals that will normally register with the person that you are not buying his story (comments, etc.).

Specific ways for the interviewer to register his reluctance to believe what has been said to him would include:

1. Facial expression that signals disagreement (such as a frown or questioning look)
2. Body lean toward rear (not the leaning forward – most attentive stance)
3. Excessive eye blinks (compared to interviewee's)
 4. Slightly rub or scratch face or head.

These techniques work very well for the three learning modalities: visual, auditory and kinesthetic.   Although people use all three of these avenues of sensation (sight, hearing, touch), each person will have a primary or preferred modality.   If you (the interviewer) can identify the primary modality used by the specific job seeker, you can then ask questions and make statements that will appeal to that particular preferred mode of learning and processing information.

The sensory learning styles have approximately the following representations for our population: Visual: 60%, Auditory: 20% and Kinesthetic: 20%.

Visual – A **visual** person likes to process new information when it is visually illustrated. He prefers to use sight to learn how to do something new. The interviewer could reinforce statements by saying "I see what you are telling me." Since his personal experiences have been processed through his eye sight, the interviewer should emphasize questions and statements that will appeal to that modality.

Auditory – An **auditory** person prefers to hear explanations and process information via the spoken word. "I hear what you mean." would be a statement that would indicate this is his preferred sensation for processing life's encounters such as various jobs, etc. It is amazing that generations of children were and are being educated by lectures in the classroom by the teacher or instructor and only about 20% prefer that method of learning! Think of how much more could be accomplished if the other two methods (visual and kinesthetic) were evenly distributed throughout the learning experiences! When interviewing this person, ask him to relate his experiences through sounds, words, feelings, etc.

Kinesthetic – A **kinesthetic** person prefers hands on experiences and will relate to conversation where "actions speak louder than words." This person processes new information best when it involves touch or manipulation. During the job interviewing session, listen (and watch the psychomotor reactions) to the interviewee as he will be expressing himself with descriptors such as "It just feels right to me."

By being aware of these three major sensory modalities, the interviewer will be able to identify the best way to communicate with any interviewee.

> **Sensory learning styles have approximately the following representations for our population:**
>
> **Visual   60%**
> **Auditory 20%**
> **Kinesthetic 20%**

Now, the ball is in your court, what are YOU going to do with the information you just read? You have choices. You can do nothing and still not present yourself as that best applicant or best interviewing supervisor. Or you can apply some of the proven interviewing and detection of deception techniques to make yourself a standout in your profession. The choice is yours; you have free will, what is your decision?

Notes............Thoughts............Ideas

_____

_____

_____

_____

_____

_____

_____

_____

_____

_____

_____

Chapter Four – Barriers and How to Remove Them

Describe examples of common actions or behaviors that could be perceived as being authoritarian in nature.

Every person is unique and has developed a personal value system based on particular _____,

_____, _____, and _____.

List some of the gaps that might be hindering a job interviewing session.

What are some verbal barriers a job interviewer might make that can impede the interviewing session?

One of the primary barriers to cross cultural communications is

_____.

Why will knowledge of other world cultures allow the interviewer to more effectively interact with those not from his own culture?

Explain how anger can be a major barrier to effective communications.

How can mirroring an interviewee's behavior improve the counseling situation?

Describe the **chocolate covered peanut concept** and create some embedded questions.

List the percentages for the sensory learning styles: Visual - _____, Auditory - _____, and Kinesthetic - _____.

What is my decision pertaining to applying the learned information from this book?

Notes.............Thoughts.............Ideas

_____

_____

_____

_____

_____

_____

_____

_____

_____

_____

REFERENCES

134

American Psychiatric Association. (2005). <u>Diagnostic and Statistical Manual of Mental Disorders</u> (Fourth Ed., Text Rev.), Washington, DC.